For my oldest daughter, Alexis, I would move mountains for you if I could, I love you with all my heart.

I was born and now I see, why can't I hear you Momma?

A little girl born hard of hearing, a mother confused and wondering why? Her little girl, it made her cry. To hurt for her and to feel her pain, the little girl won't hear again. I cried and cried but didn't hear, the sound of my own voice calling her, calling my mom who was always there, her touch calmed me down from all my fears.

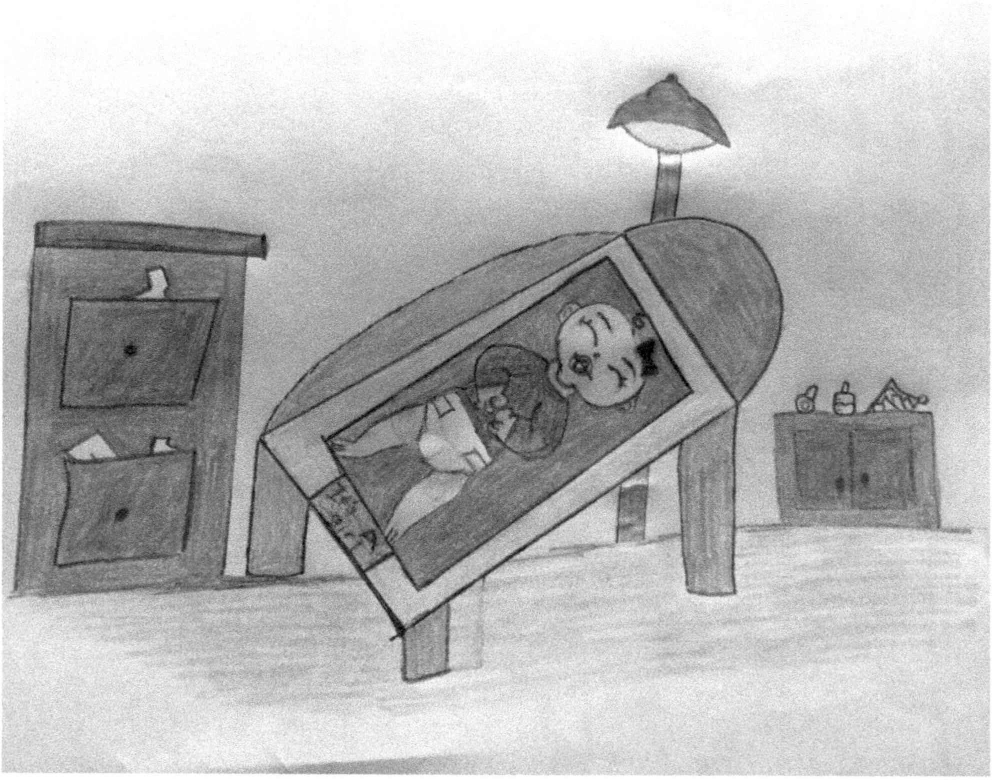

4

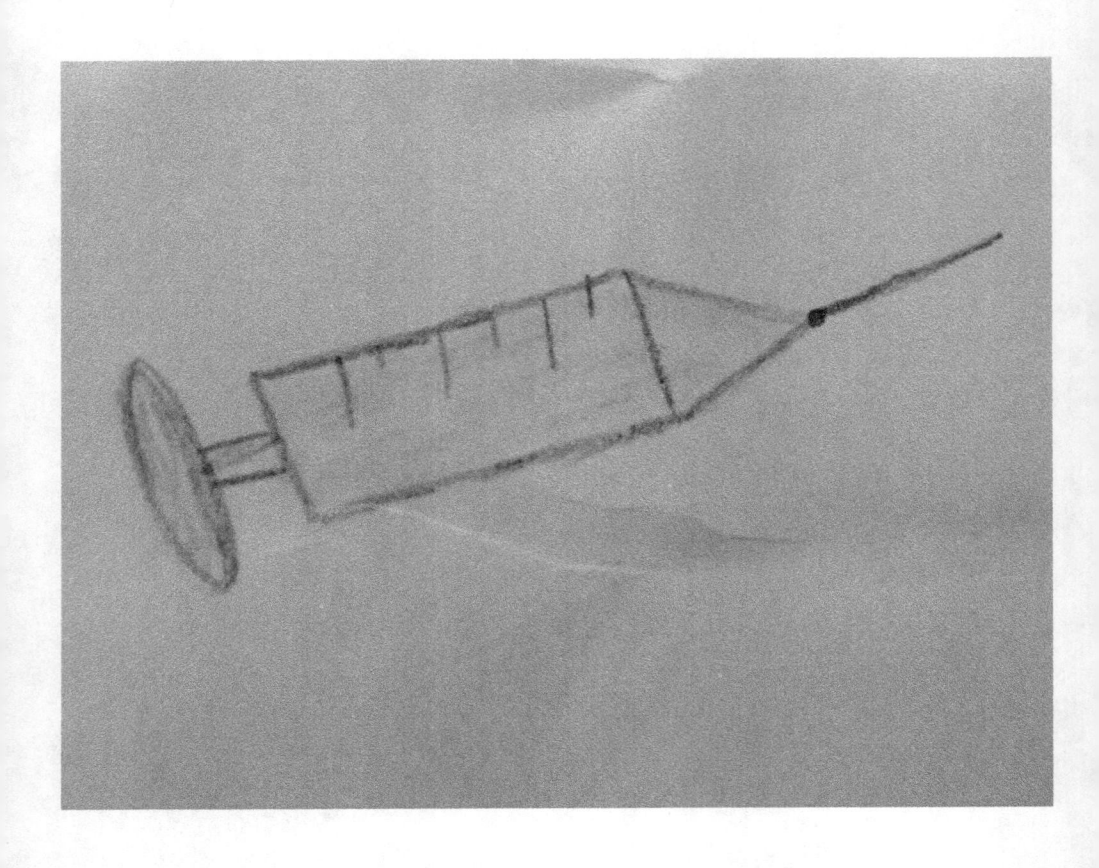

Today I went to a weird and scary place, the walls were all the same a thousands faces, but only one which made me smile, my mothers face a quiet sound. I cried again from the pain I got, " I feel so bad my baby's first shot", I didn't know what was going on, a soothing voice I would never hear but the smile on her face she kept me near. I see her smile and felt just right , I would hold my mother close and tight.

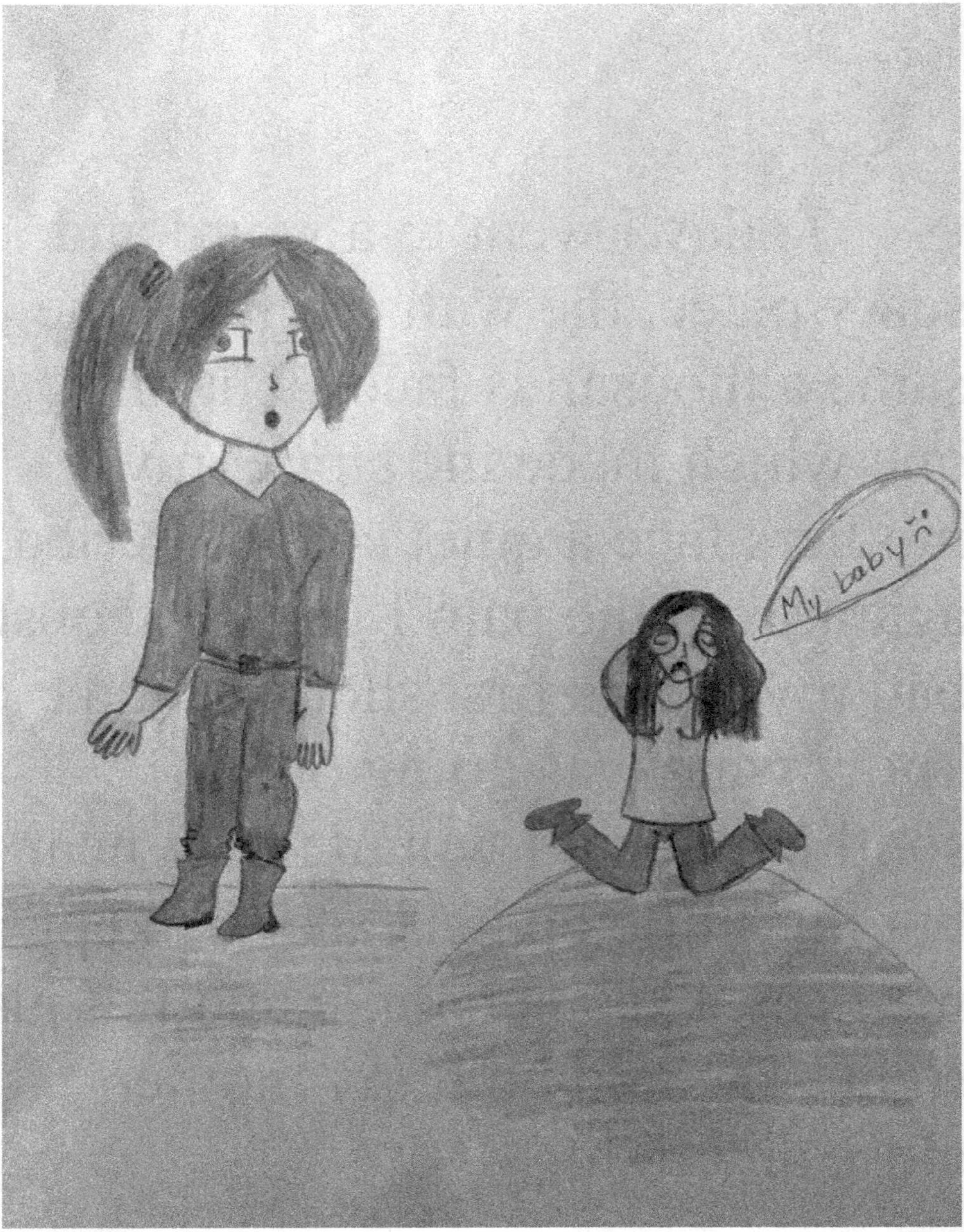
My baby

My time in life seem to go on forever, from one doctor to another, one shot, one test, this was my life but it was the best because that same smile, kept me together.

"Why does she have to go through all of this?" Mothered cried, I didn't know what it was or how she felt inside. My daughter is hurting and I can't help, I continue to smile for her and myself. I want to cure her broken parts, I will fill her with love since it is all I got.

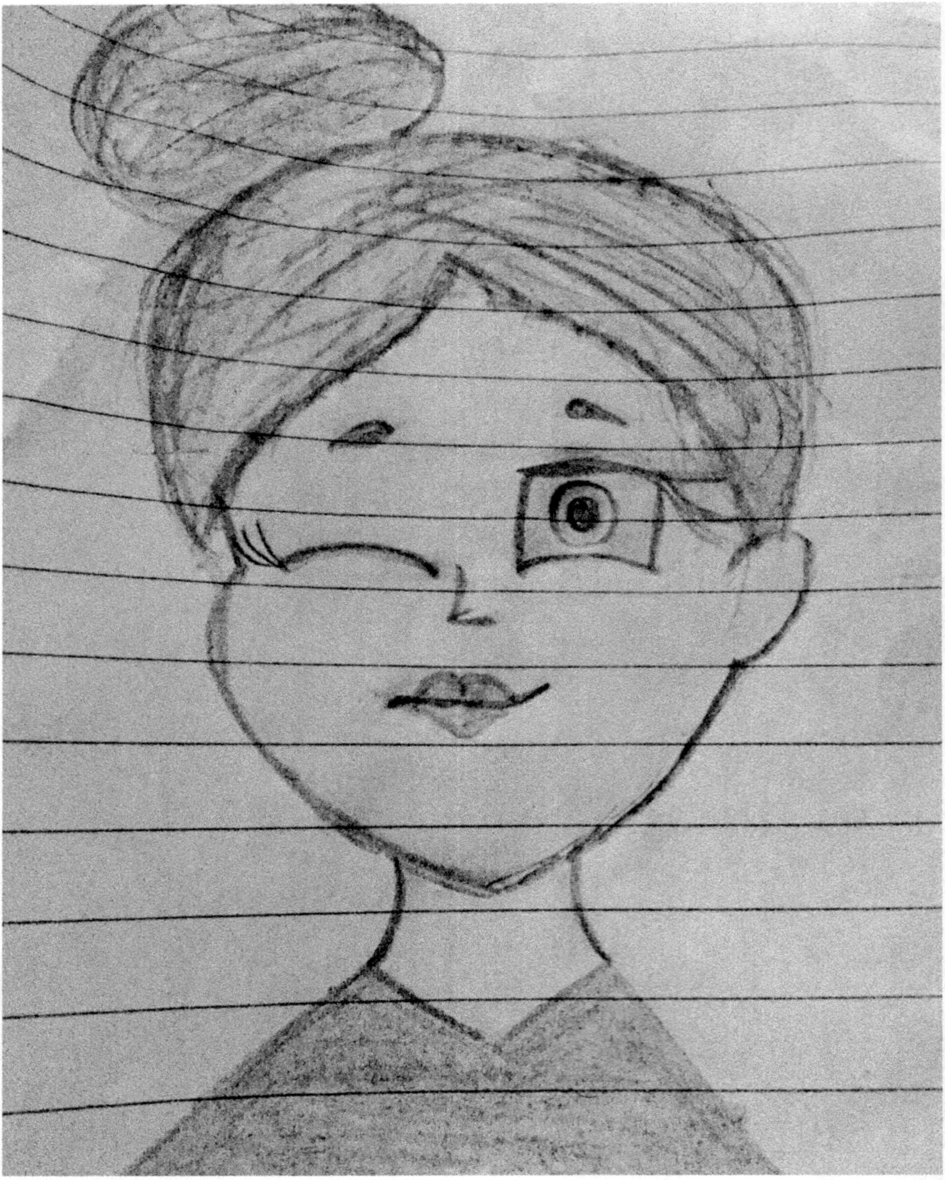

I grew older and had all I could ever want, everything I touched my mother bought, if I looked at it it became mine, since I didn't talk I just whined, and when I whined my mother gave, all she had she saved and saved. Every birthday big and full, of family, friends and presents too. I didn't know what was going on, my bubble grew bigger as I grew and grew strong, my mother never showed that anything was wrong.

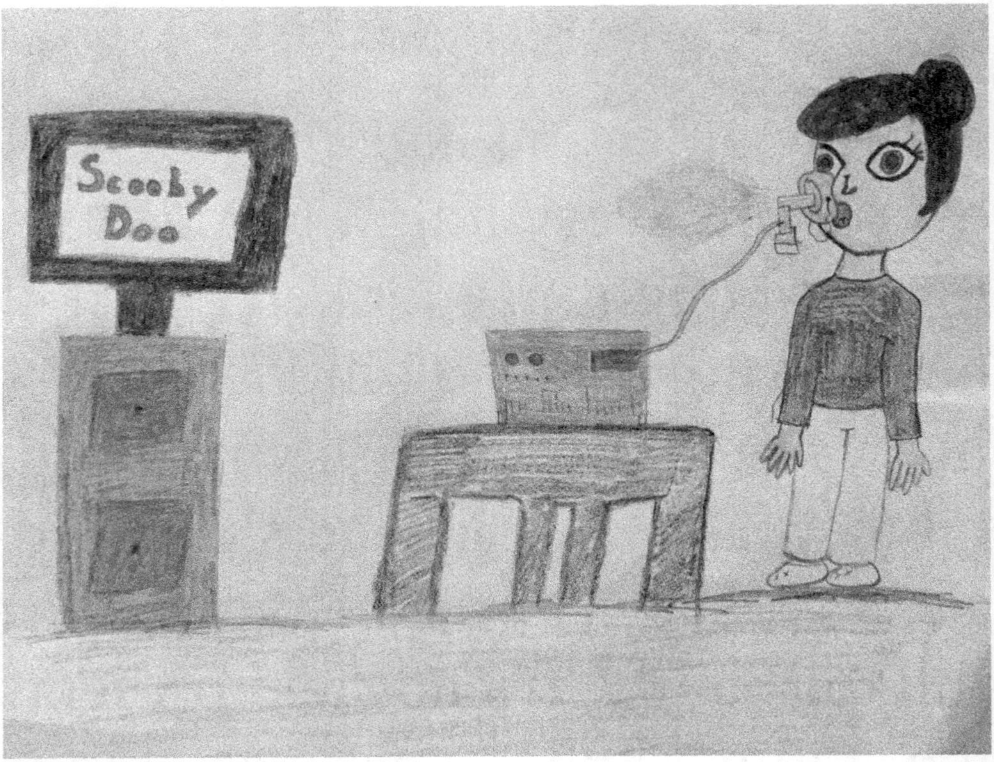
Scooby
Doo

I quickly learned all I needed to know to help my daughter get out from that bubble. What was wrong and what was right, I still didn't have all the answers, searched day and night. I tried one thing then I tried two, I was lost to what I should do. At age 2 she got RSV a virus that makes it hard to breath. It started with asthma which affected her lungs from breathing well, only time will tell, what else would go wrong or what would go right, I tried and tried to make it alright. This little girl went completely deaf, I found a device that will help with that, but *first* I learned of all the facts.

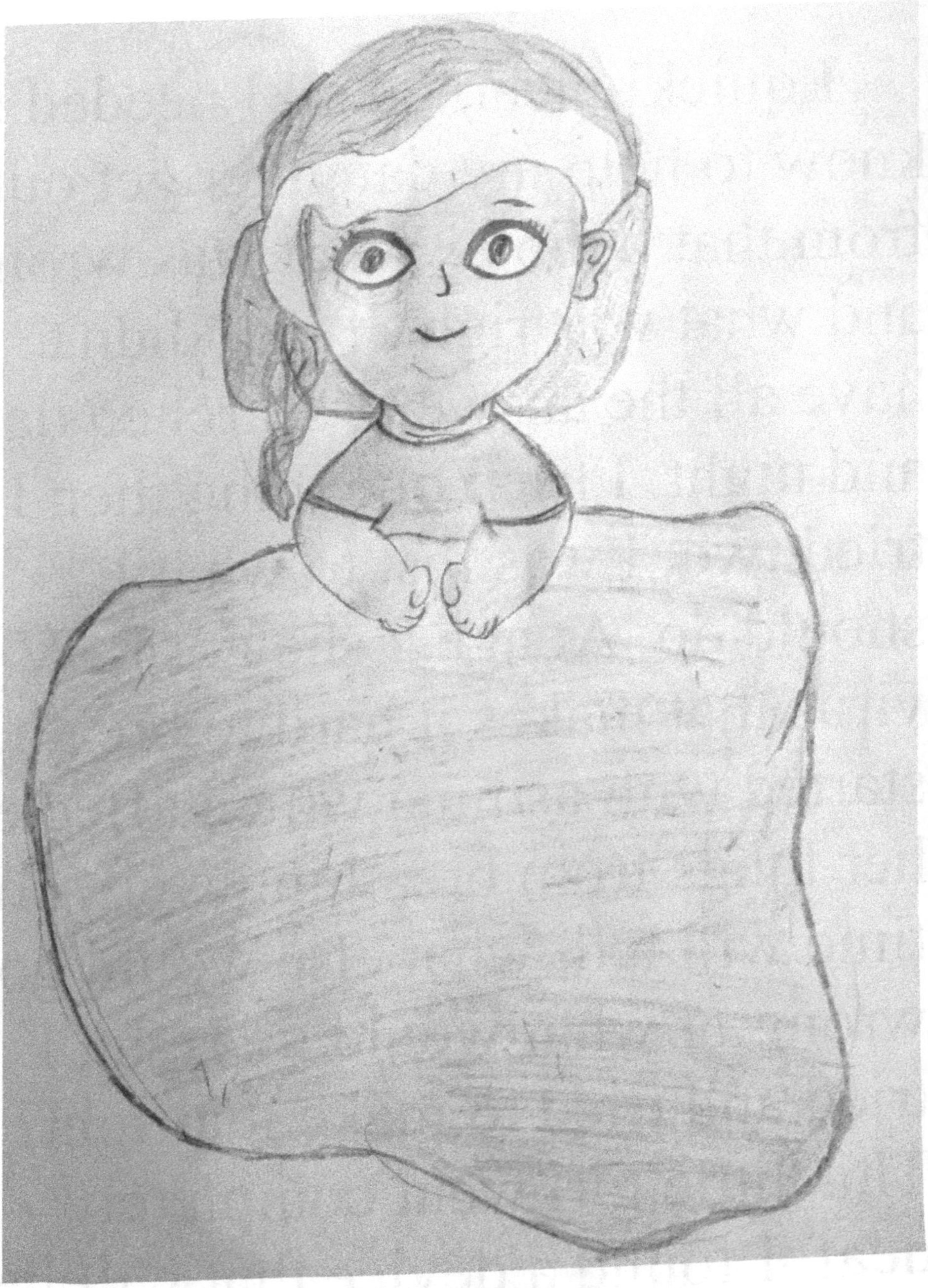

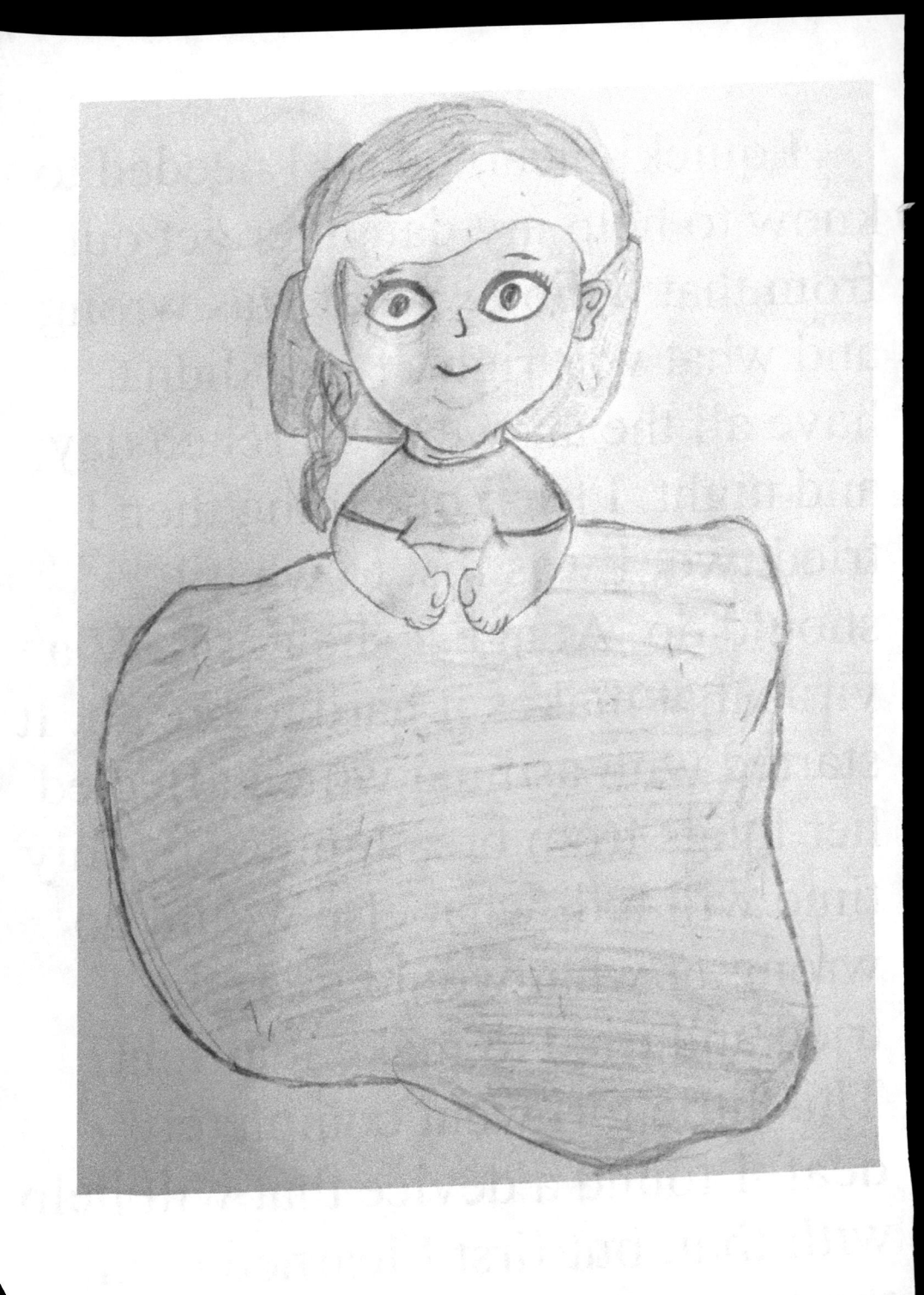

I went to sleep in a weird place, had people with mask and a bed that shakes, it rolls and moves and they took me for a ride, I went to sleep or did I die? I woke up and touched my head, I had a bandage it covered my ear but there goes that smile it didn't disappear. My mother was there her face made me laugh, my bubble was safe she's here at last.

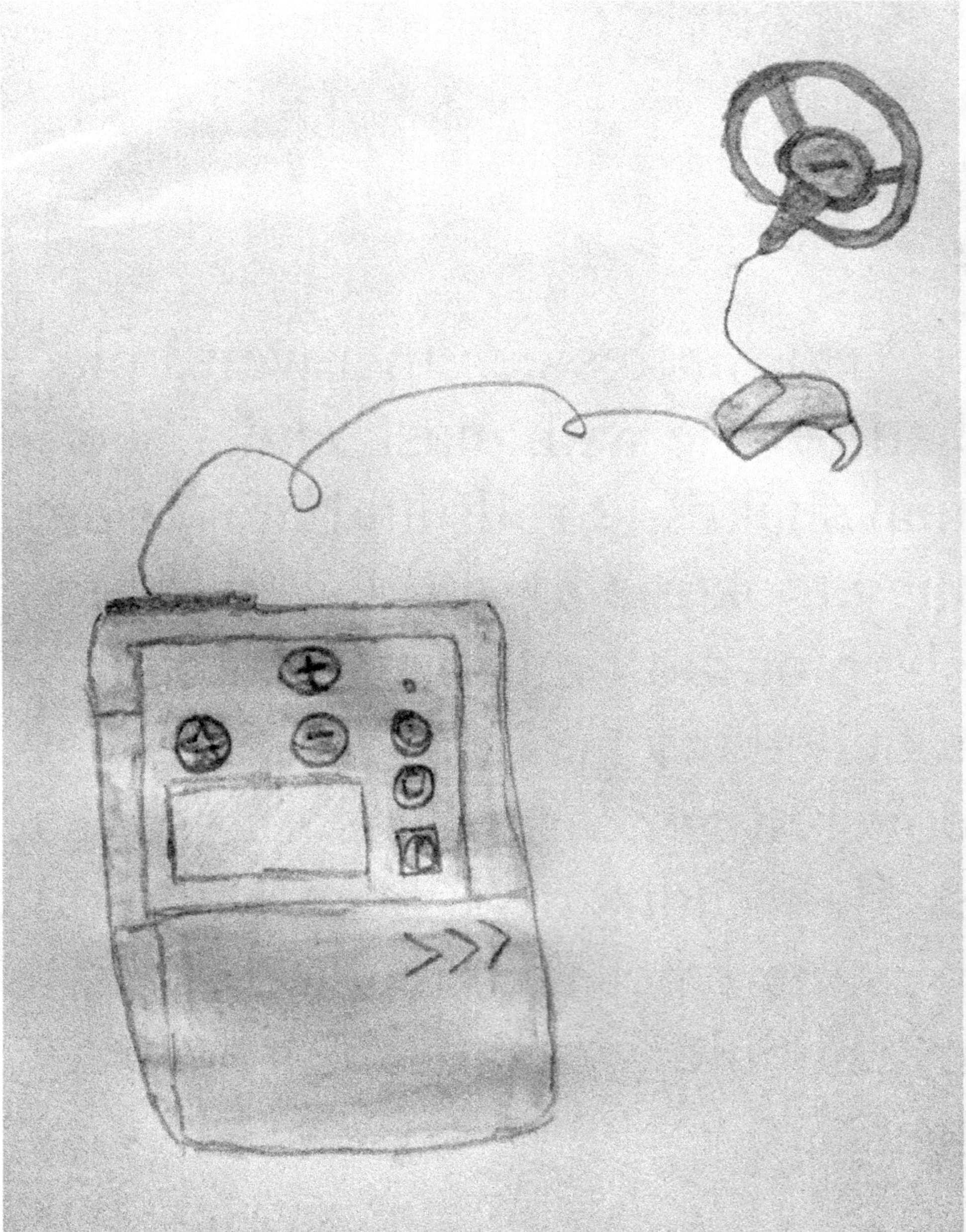

My baby got fitted for a cochlear implant, a device that helps her to hear what she can't. Year after year and doctor after doctor, my daughter grew up and she got stronger, the device helped a little but not a lot, she still couldn't tell me what she wants. I never got to hear her voice, her tell me she loved me I had no choice, I still smiled each and every day, gave her all my love anyway.

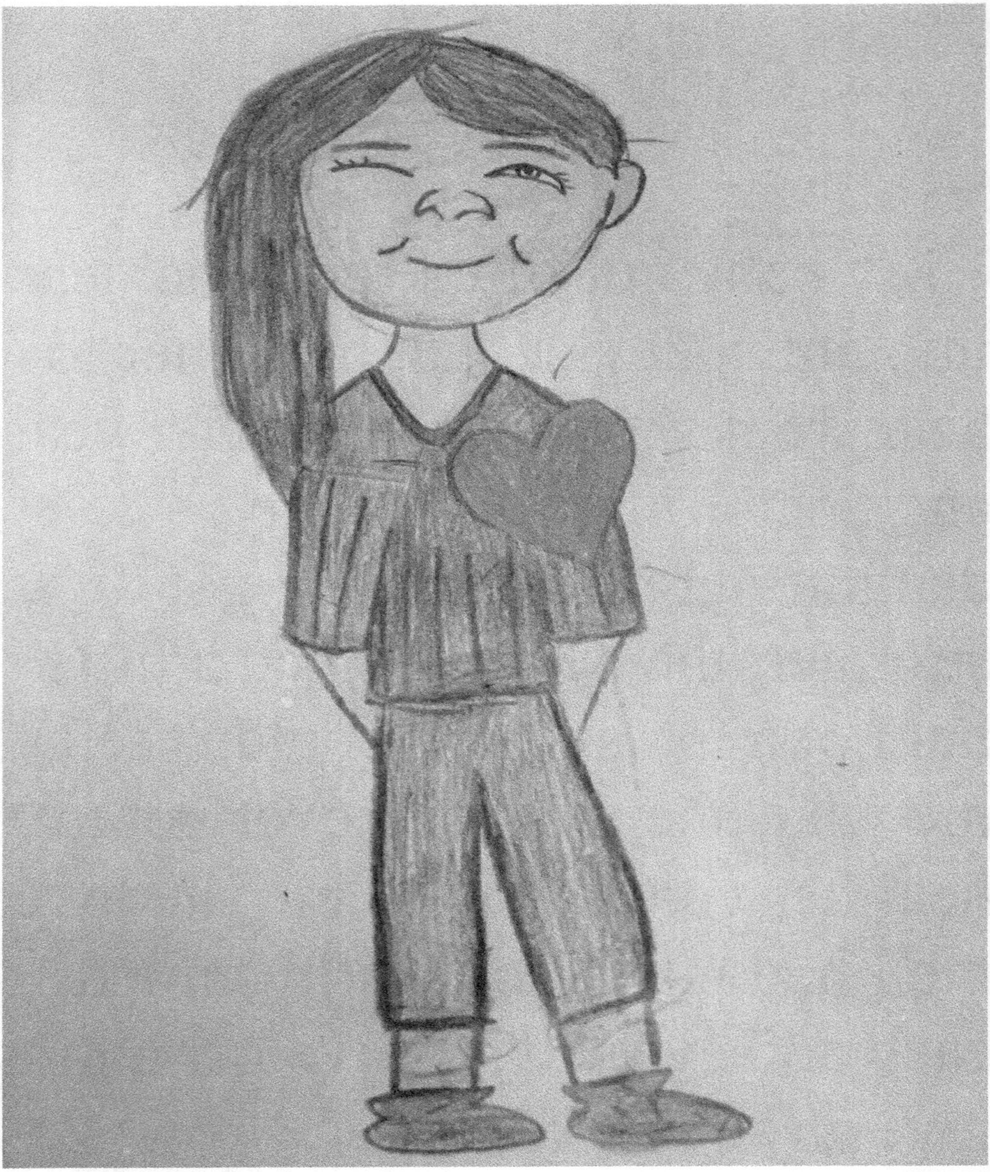

For this little girl did not know a thing, but was filled with love deep within, she stood in her bubble for it grew bigger every year, this little girl would never hear, she'll never talked or knew what was going on, but she will love for her love is strong.

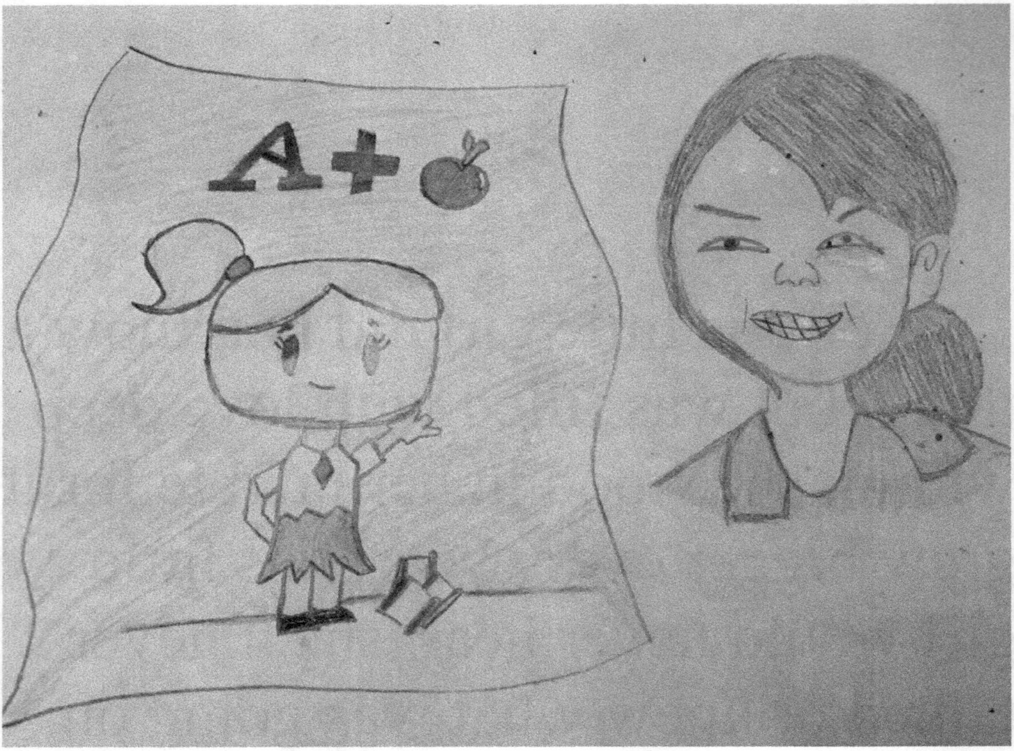
A+

I now live in another place, I got to strong and very upset, I got older and couldn't talk, there was things I needed, things I want. I couldn't tell them how I felt, I was locked in my bubble with no one else. My mothers face cried many tears it made me angry it made me fear, for I didn't know what was going wrong, my mother couldn't do it she wasn't strong. I still got love when she sent me away there was no difference things were the same.

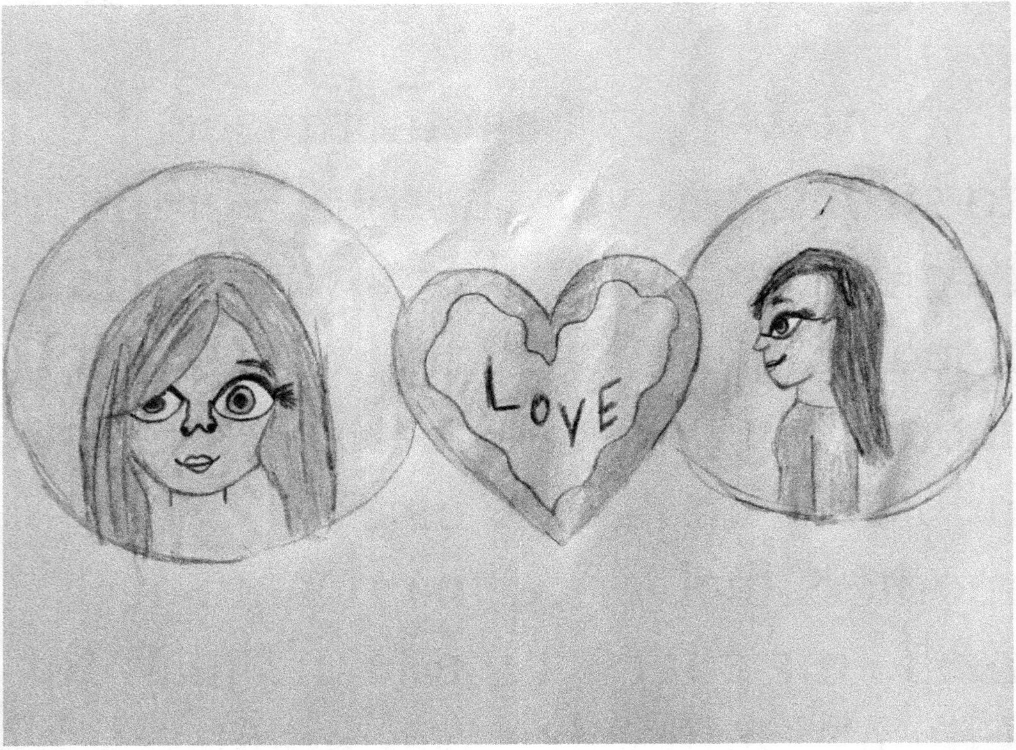
LOVE

My mother came to see me all the time, the love she had it still was mine. My life has changed, I've learned a lot, most I do by routine but I've got a lot. There's people here I call them friends, I'm still in the bubble that I was in. I still feel loved for she's always there, my mother I take everywhere. When I'm alone and when I fear her smile will make it disappear.

For I can't join her but I will always try, she makes me hurt but makes me smile, for the love I have for her is like no one else, a mothers love will always work.

24